WILLIAM WALTON

arr. Robert Gower

ORB AND SCEPTRE

Coronation March, 1953

MUSIC DEPARTMENT

OXFORD

UNIVERSITY PRESS

Orb and Sceptre

(Coronation March, 1953)

WILLIAM WALTON
arr. Robert Gower

* Passages in square brackets may be played on a solo reed.

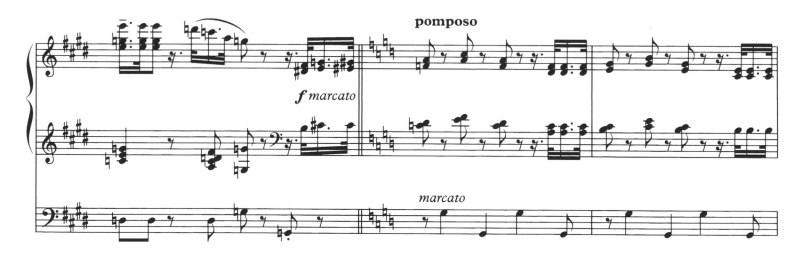

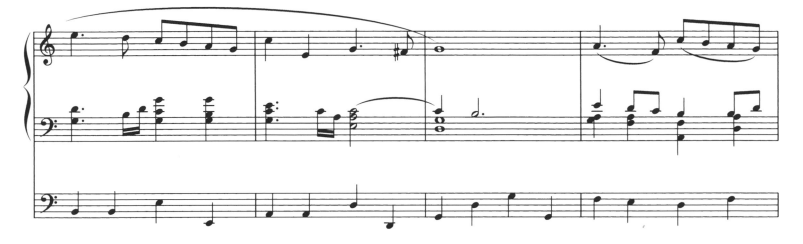

maestoso

Come prima

D.S. al ⊕ *poi al Coda*

CODA

Largamente

ff molto legato

subito vivace

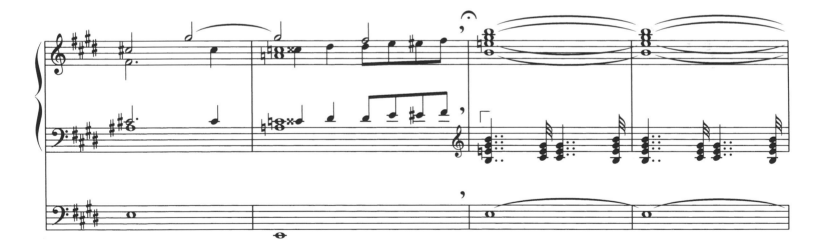

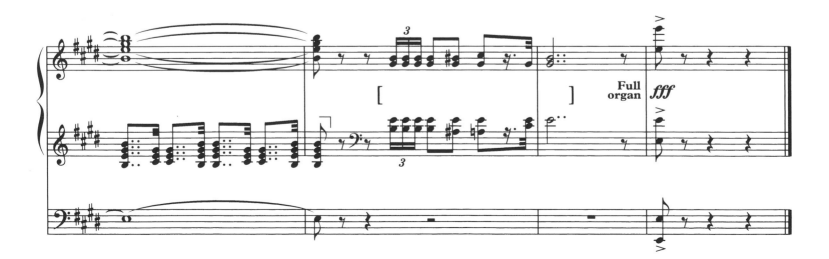